NEW DANCE

Writings on Modern Dance

Doris Humphrey

NEW DANCE

Writings on Modern Dance

DORIS HUMPHREY

Selected and edited by
Charles Humphrey Woodford

Princeton Book Company, Publishers
Hightstown, NJ

Composition, cover and interior design by Elizabeth Helmetsie

Publisher's Cataloging-In-Publication Data
(Prepared by The Donohue Group, Inc.)

Humphrey, Doris, 1895–1958.
New dance : writings on modern dance / Doris Humphrey ; selected and edited by Charles Humphrey Woodford.
p. ; cm.

Includes bibliographical references.
ISBN: 978–0–87127–307–9

1. Modern dance. 2. Choreography. I. Woodford, Charles Humphrey. II. Title.

GV1783 .H83 2008
793.3

Princeton Book Company, Publishers
614 Route 130
Hightstown, NJ 08520
www.dancehorizons.com

CONTENTS

Part 2:

NOTES ON DANCES 71

INTRODUCTION

New Dance (1935) was one of Doris Humphrey's most innovative dances, combining a visionary social theme with symphonic group choreography. "New dance" could also describe the whole era of movement and choreographic exploration in the late 1920s and 1930s that became known as American modern dance. Doris Humphrey, along with her partner Charles Weidman, and Martha Graham are its founders.

The collection of Doris Humphrey's dance writings and notes on specific dances presents her principles of technique and composition and shows the application of her theories to choreography. A few of these writings have appeared elsewhere, notably in *Doris Humphrey: An Artist First,* the autobiography edited and completed by Selma Jeanne Cohen, but most are published here for the first time.

The selection is intended to be focused rather than comprehensive. The first part, *Principles,* is loosely chronological to show the development of ideas. The second part, *Notes on Dances,* is in chronological order, but represents only dances for which Humphrey's own descriptions could be found (the exception being Letitia Ide's interpretation of her role in *Day on Earth*). For some dances there were extensive notes, but for others only a single line.

Editing has been done to avoid redundancy and in certain places to improve style, clarify meaning, avoid anachronisms and eliminate digressions. I am sure that my mother would not mind my taking these liberties in order to bring her thoughts and work to the attention of contemporary readers.

Charles Humphrey Woodford

NOTE

Long before I understood movement and gesture I had an inescapable urge to compose—or to be exact, I had a passion for directing people in moving groups. I do not pretend that, in the early stages, I wanted to say anything in particular. I had only an abounding joy in dance, and especially in many people dancing together. I still think this is the *sine qua non* for dances, it's as simple as that. Do you love to dance? And for choreographers, do you love to see someone else moving according to your dream? For those who aspire to direct groups, do you respond intensely to masses of people at baseball games and parades and processions? Do you like folk dances, and what do you feel when you see birds wheeling together?

Doris Humphrey

ACKNOWLEDGMENTS

A special thank you to my wife, Connie Woodford, for her editorial help in preparing the manuscript by turning notes and ideas into a book, as well as for her discriminating sense of form in expression and design.

For their assistance in researching and providing material I am indebted to Jenny Dahmus of The Juilliard School Library, Betsy Miller of the Limón Dance Foundation, Minos G. Nicolas, Executive Director of the Doris Humphrey Institute and Charles Perrier of the Jerome Robbins Dance Division, Library for the Performing Arts of the New York Public Library.

My assistant, Marcia Sylvester, suggested what should have been obvious to me: that I dedicate this book to Doris Humphrey's great-granddaughters, for this is part of their heritage.

Charles Humphrey Woodford

DEDICATION

For Finlay and Chloe Jennings,
Doris Humphrey's great-granddaughters

Part 1

PRINCIPLES

1

My Approach to Modern Dance

Declaration

My dance is an art concerned with human values. It upholds only those values that make for harmony and opposes all forces inimical to those values. In part, its movement may be used for decoration, entertainment, emotional release or technical display; but primarily it is composed as an expression of American life as I see it today.

This new dance of action comes inevitably from the people who had to subdue a continent, to make a thousand paths through forest and plain, to conquer the mountains, and eventually to raise up towers of steel and glass. The American dance is born of this new world, new life and new vigor.

I believe that the dancer belongs to his time and place and that he can only express that which passes through or close to his experience. The one indispensable quality in a work of art is a consistent point of view related to the times. When this is lost, and when there is substituted for it an aptitude for putting together bits of this and that drawn from extraneous material and dead methods, there can be no integrity.

Since my dance is concerned with immediate human values, my basic technique lies in the natural movements of the body. One cannot express contemporary life without humanizing movement, as distinguished from the dehumanization of the ballet. The modern dancer must come down from the points to the bare foot in order to establish his human relation to gravity and reality.

I wish my dance to reflect some experience of my own in relationship to the outside world; to be based on reality illumined by imagination; to be organic rather than synthetic; to call forth a definite reaction from my audience; and to make its contribution toward the drama of life.

Principles of movement

I conceive movement, for the dancer's purpose, to be basically one of equilibrium. In fact, *my entire technique consists of the development of the process of falling away from and returning to equilibrium.* This is far more than a mere business of "keeping your balance," which is a muscular and structural problem. Falling and recovering is the very stuff of movement, the constant flux that is going on in every living body, in all its tiniest parts, all the time.

Nor is this all, for the process has a psychological meaning as well. I recognized these emotional overtones very early and instinctively responded very strongly to the exciting danger of the fall, and the repose and peace of the recovery. Only much later did I find in Nietzsche a word expression of the meaning of these movements which revealed to me the fundamental rightness of my feeling. His two basic *kinds* of men, the *Apollonian* and the *Dionysian*, forever opposed and existing both in one man and in groups of men, are the symbols of man's struggle for progress on one hand, and his desire for stability on the other hand. These are not only the basis of Greek tragedy, as Nietzsche pointed out, but of all dramatic movement, particularly dance. And dance movement should be fundamentally dramatic, that is to say, *human*, not decorative, geometric or mechanical.

The technique evolved out of this theory is amazingly rich in possibilities. Beginning with simple falls complete to the floor and recoveries to standing, many elements of movements reveal themselves in addition to the falling of the body in space. One of these is *rhythm*. In a series of falls and recoveries, accents occur which establish a rhythm, even a phrase, as the time-space is varied due to gravitational pull on the mass of the body.

Another element is *dynamism*, that is, changes of intensity.

A third element is *design*. Even the latter, usually considered to be linear, having nothing to do with movement, is a functional result of the body's compensatory changes.

If left to itself, the body will make a number of weight adjustments in the course of a fall; and each of these will describe a design in space. I call these compensatory movements *oppositions*, and they occur in partial falls as well as in complete ones. For example, one foot will step forward to save the body on its way down. At the same time, the arms will swing out. This is also true in walking, *which is a partial fall*. Each one of these elementary parts of movement is capable of more or less isolation and almost limitless variation.

Extension of movement into studies

In addition to the purely technical development in dance which these insights led to, there was, all the while, the growing discovery that these movements were satisfying, even exciting to do and to see—not pure abstractions in the sense that technique is an abstraction, but had content. Because they sprang so truly and psychologically from physical life, they were emotionally stirring even without a program. This characteristic led me to compose a number of dance studies and even dance compositions entirely without a dramatic idea. Indeed, I think sometimes that the composer's meaning can only be conveyed fully by movement.

In the future, when America is finally won over to modern dance, audiences will enjoy the drama of life in motion as they now enjoy the drama of life in abstract music. Sometimes, however, the dance composer wishes to say something which demands specific treatment as to time and place and people. Here I use the same technical equipment; but all the movements, themes, phrases—in short, all the material of the dramatic dance—are conditioned by the idea to be expressed. Whereas we begin technically with natural movements resulting from fall and recovery that tend always toward the ideal, these same movements will be changed and distorted on being subjected to drama, which frequently demands less than the ideal or struggle for it.

This is the real explanation of the angular patterns which have come to be bywords of modern dance. The dancer cannot be concerned entirely with the graceful line nor even with the fine animal ease with which technical study can and does provide him, because he is a living being, played upon by life, bursting with opinions and compulsions to express them. Sometimes, not always, he is concerned with themes of strife, struggle, and oppression. These demand an acrid line, a steely quality not found in purely kinetic movement unconditioned by ideas.

Body mechanics and technical studies

To dance well, technical mastery of the body is the first prerequisite. And since my dance grows out of natural bodily movement, training for it must involve natural movements. The following brief outline will indicate proper procedures:

A. Body mechanics

1. *Stretches*

   The body must be prepared for greater than natural strength, suppleness, endurance and coordination. This involves relaxing body bends; isolation exercises for separate parts of the body; exercises especially for the feet, Achilles tendon, knee and thigh muscles to insure greater power in elevation; stretching for the legs, and stretching the torso for the development of the abdominal walls.

2. *Walks, runs, jumps and leaps*

   These are fundamental *natural* movements of all persons. For the dancer, they are a basic vocabulary that he uses to express his ideas and communicate what is within him to others. I concentrate on natural form in walking, running, jumping and leaping, so that the dancer's expressions may be true and sincere.

B. Dance studies

1. *First series of falls*

   These are simple complete falls and recoveries in four directions. They give balance and control in every position of the body, the basic movements in relation to gravity.

2. *Second series of falls*

   When the first simple falls have been fairly well mastered, I give students a more elaborate and difficult series. Preparatory movements are developed. The falls require more strength and control. Falls are in four directions. They are essentially dynamic studies.

3. *Design studies*

   There are three kinds of design in my dance. To explain them requires a knowledge of choreography too involved to explain here. [1]

4. *Studies in contrasts of design and dynamics*

5. *Variations*

   Combinations of all elements are conceived and performed, with stress on rhythms.

[1] See Ernestine Stodelle, *The Dance Technique of Doris Humphrey and Its Creative Potential.*

[2] See Doris Humphrey, *The Art of Making Dances*, chapters 6–10 for a complete discussion of design.

2

Breath Rhythm

Breath rhythm is the one principle of all movement, whether actuated by emotional ritual or physical or intellectual impetus. Breath rhythm in the time sense is a two-part phrase, the first longer than the second; in the space sense, a filling and expanding followed by a contraction; in the dynamic sense, a continuous movement growing in tension, followed by a letting go of tension which finishes with an accent.

By combining these three elements of the breath rhythm consciously in various ways the whole of the dance may be evolved.

3
Invitation to the Dancer

It was inevitable that in a country like this, where physical activity has been so important in its upbuilding and where sports have an honored and important place, that a new dance form, indigenous and unique, should have been developed.

The modern American dance could have sprung from no other soil. It has appeared in the long history of the world's dance experiences in answer to the particular temperamental needs of this country and this time. However, each one of the leaders of American dance has his own approach, his own ideas as to which of the characteristics of our times is significant and important. As [my partner] Charles Weidman and I see it, the dance should be direct, dynamic, friendly; sometimes humorous, gay, impudent, at other times profound, intense, with a social conscience.

Dance is the only activity that can employ all the faculties of a human being at once, including the emotions and the mind. Little does the audience realize what a feat of mental concentration and memory it can be to dance a complicated work in broken rhythms, counterpointed against an accompaniment and against other groups on the stage, while at the same time having to project the essential emotion of the piece. Dance is the only physical activity to combine rhythm, pattern of the whole, subtle conscious form, and meaning. The art dance, that is—other types: dancing for entertainment, for technical display, for fun (folk dancing), for emotional release or for decoration—need not concern themselves with meaning. But in the hands of an artist, dance can be and has been of a stature to measure with that of any other art.

Modern dance has been accused of being remote and difficult. Our dance need not be a cult of unintelligibility, an esoteric enterprise with never a crack through which a gleam of humor can enter, an exercise in aloofness. By its very origins it is dedicated to an expression of life as a whole, today; it can and must involve itself closely with its audience in a mutual exploration of that complicated but fascinating territory.

Now, the dancer's experience is in large part the audience's experience as well since the material of dance composition is taken from the same common fund of living. In addition, the average American, with his love of sports, is almost sure to have an acquaintance with some form of physical activity. These two facts alone are sufficient preparation for "understanding" modern dance, if the layman will put aside his fear that everything in the program is going to be unintelligible. His own physical activity has already awakened the kinesthetic sense by which movement is understood in its own terms, immediately by the body; and the dances themselves, based on familiar human material, have merely been stylized and given new form. A little application to the acceptance of those theatrical conventions in which modern dance is clothed, and the layman is ready to receive a rich new artistic experience.

In the words of an English critic, "We are needing to get the delight which belongs to the dancer out of all the processes of living, which should be detailed and sharp, impinging straight on the nerve, without the eternal stress of the inhibiting intellect." On the other hand, dancers have the responsibility of making sure that they really have a fresh approach to living in their offerings, not just a technical display, or themes and movements remote from common experience.

Let the dancer constantly ask himself, "Is this a design for living?"

4

Interview: Teaching Composition

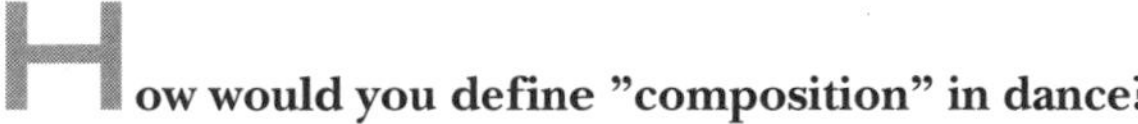

How would you define "composition" in dance?

DH: Composition is, simply, the art of composing dances.

What do you consider the main elements, or essentials, of composition?

DH: Form, content and execution:

Form includes (a) rhythm, (b) design and (c) dynamics. These are the elements out of which you make the movements but not, however, the composition. An understanding of rhythm, and a mastery of its many different uses in dance, is essential for the dancer. For instance, rhythm can be emotional, dramatic or metric; it can be simple (in the use of single rhythms) or complex (the use of two or more different rhythms together).

Design in dance includes all of those elements that use space, such as focus, direction, level. There are many different kinds of space patterns—square, zig-zag, diagonal, round, straight, side-to-side.

Most students have a hazy understanding of stage design and the use of stage space.

The dynamic of a movement is the particular quality of the movement, smooth or sharp, sustained or percussive. The use of two different dynamics in the same movement (in different parts of the body) is one means of varying and heightening movement. There is in addition to the space design mentioned above, a space dynamic.

Content in dance is that which is danced about.

Execution is the manner in which a dance is performed, the quality of the technical rendering as well as the projection of the content of the dance.

What means do you use to make students conscious of and skilled in these elements in composition?

DH: Through discussion of examples from my own repertoire, which serve as illustration (sections and movements which are actually learned by students) and brief studies composed by each student (or group of students) in the use of the basic tools or elements, of composition—rhythm, dynamics, design.

What do you feel should be the relation between physical technique and composition?

DH: Beginners should by all means have composition, if for no other reason than the psychological one, of avoiding blocks regarding creative work in dance.

How would you define "content" as related to composition? Would you distinguish it from subject matter?

DH: Content seems to me to include subject matter in the sense of dramatic idea.

Do you analyze "content," "subject matter" in your classes?

DH: Yes, particularly do I insist that students clarify in their own minds "that which they are dancing about," the progress of their idea as revealed in their dance (its beginning, development and conclusion). Also I stress the necessity of looking for the *action* inherent in an idea, and of avoiding those subjects for dance that have little or no action in them. A dance should have progressive change and growth. An audience should be able to see something "happen" to the participants between its opening and its close. This is a general literary and artistic principle. I caution students to consider the dance as a whole, and what they wish to say in it, its end and evolvement toward same. They then have a sounding board for the testing and selection of each new movement, which should be considered in the light of the total dance and development of its idea. This is not to say, however, that a dance cannot change as it progresses, and as you discover new movements and impulses; but its whole meaning will hardly alter, and should be definite in the composer's mind.

What do you feel are the major problems students face in handling subject matter?

DH: Lack of action within the idea selected. These mistakes are also common: weakness of movement due to an inadequacy in the subject matter chosen; failure to crystallize the idea and its development; failure in motivation, or identification with the subject chosen.

Do you think there are any subjects difficult or impossible to treat in dance; or subjects particularly difficult for a beginner to handle?

DH: Yes. Literary themes (such as a story) for the beginner are difficult. In attempting any subject that is too specific and concrete, the beginner (who has not learned or had sufficient experience with abstracting movement from such sources) invariably handles it realistically.

How would you define "form" in dance?

DH: Form is the overall design of a composition. The elements listed previously are used in the development of themes within the total "form."

What emphasis do you put upon "form" in your classes?

DH: Students should have practice in completing studies in form, brief enough to allow them to get experience in handling the many different forms in dance, such as the A B A, cumulative, repetitive, broken, recurring.

What particular dance "forms" (styles) do you teach in your composition class?

DH: I use forms such as those listed above, the various musical forms (like theme and variations) but I teach no specific "styles." Students are free to compose within any idiom that they might choose.

What relation does "form" in dance have to "form" in the other arts?

DH: The elements and principles involved in creative work in the other arts are very similar to those in dance, which is inevitably linked with the arts of music, theater, painting and sculpture.

What methods, in general, do you use in teaching the elements listed above—the use of space, rhythm, design and style in composition?

DH: The general methods used predominantly in my teaching are discussion, demonstration and practice (in composing studies using the different tools of composition already mentioned.)

How do you approach the use of those forms you listed above, for beginners?

DH: The same steps are involved as those above; but always choreography class is a laboratory, and the most important learning is that of actual participation—either in following movements which illustrate a principle or in trying to solve problems in solo or group studies. Taking part in the dances of other students and seeing each other's work sharpens the critical eye and is an important aspect of the class.

What place do you feel that random improvisation has as an approach to composition? In what way do you use it in your own classes?

DH: I do not use it. Occasionally I ask students to improvise on a theme. Improvisation to music I have done only with children. Perhaps it is all right with older students if they are not too inhibited to really take part. It is good as an emotional release.

What is your opinion of pantomime and dramatic action as sources for dance movement?

DH: I think both are wonderful as long as they are translated into movement, the danger being, of course, that the transition remains incomplete. Done by a master, I like pantomime.

How do you teach the use of pantomime and gesture as a basis for abstraction of movement?

DH: There are several different sources of gesture: social, religious, conventional, racial and national. I teach their use by the assignment of specific studies. I sometimes ask for a study in "silent conversation," or a similar subject that affords the use of many different gestures. A gesture, abstracted, can also become a theme, varied in rhythm, dynamics and space design.

Do you find that dramatization of experiences and situations causes students to use naturally many of the elements of composition listed previously?

DH: No, the results of this usually turn out to be too realistic. Nearly always the student must go back and abstract from the idea movement that suggests but does not literally represent the action, idea or experience.

Do you recommend the use of stage props as a means of stimulating student in composition?

DH: I am not given to blank composing around props, but am all in favor of using them when called for. Supposedly, the genuine motivation for the kind of dance we have been discussing is experience, and related to this, the whole idea of communication. If it is possible to feel about a triangle, ruler or other object so intensely as to want to dance about it, then do so. But it is not likely to prove very fruitful.

Do you find that analogies between dance and other arts are stimulating to students in composition? And that they lead to experimentation with new forms and patterns of movement?

DH: Yes, notably literature, painting and music.

What do you feel is your main contribution to the theory of modern dance composition?

DH: The "extended" form, which allows dances to last more than three or four minutes.

What would you consider the major influence upon your own choreography, and upon your theory of dance composition?

DH: Ruth St. Denis.

What other styles of dance—ballet, theater, ethnic—have particularly influenced you?

DH: I can't say that any of these have been a particular influence.

What related arts have been most stimulating to you?

DH: Music.

What is your philosophy about the use of music for modern dance?

DH: The first precept for students, probably, is that they not take music beyond their own range in complexity. Music should not be a corset for the dance, nor yet a god to whom they dance. I always encourage students to try to escape from the piano, and explore the musical resources of other instruments and sounds. Most students are exceedingly cautious and orthodox in their use of music; they should experiment with defying musical rhythm—dancing against the metre (instead of being its servant), varying their rhythm and the music as to dominance (allowing first one, then the other, to lead) and trying counterpoint and syncopation.

Do you guide students in their choice of music for dance? If so, how?

DH: I try to show students the possibilities inherent in different kinds of accompaniment by illustrations from dances which are unusual in this respect. Students also are asked to select music for a solo or group dance they wish to work on. This music is then criticized by myself and the rest of the class as to its appropriateness for dance, possible difficulties in using it, and relation to the content of the projected dance.

What kinds of music have you found are difficult for beginners to handle?

DH: Romantic, symphonic forms, particularly; but any music that is beyond them in complexity should be avoided.

What is your opinion about the use of poetry as accompaniment for dance?

DH: I think it is most useful for dance, *if* edited.

What kinds of poetry have you found difficult or inadvisable for a beginner to use?

DH: Poetry that lacks action, or is too abstract or concerns an experience outside the range of the dancer. Also, beginning students are apt to "illustrate" poetry, to fit their movement to the words. There is no reason for the illustration, either of literature or music. Young students usually lack the experience that would enable them to deal with the basic emotions. They should steer clear of foreign forms and styles of movement. To take an extreme example, it [would be] hopeless for a young girl to portray a lonely old man.

How do you approach the problem of percussion with students?

DH: I use special studies in percussion and the use of percussive movement, and try to extend the range of percussive instruments used.

Do you find students more responsive to this form of accompaniment, in that they are more likely to experiment with rhythms if using percussion?

DH: Yes.

Do you give special studies in the use of rhythm?

DH: Yes.

5

A Personal Note on Composition

Long before I understood movement and gesture I had an inescapable urge to compose—or to be exact, I had a passion for directing people in moving groups. I do not pretend that, in the early stages, I wanted to say anything in particular. I had only an abounding joy in dance, and especially in many people dancing together. I still think this is the *sine qua non* for dances, it's as simple as that. Do you love to dance? And for choreographers, do you love to see someone else moving according to your dream? For those who aspire to direct groups, do you respond intensely to masses of people at baseball games and parades and processions? Do you like folk dances, and what do you feel when you see birds wheeling together?

Reasons for not composing or not dancing at all would be *yes* answers to: Would you rather improve your stretch than anything else? Be honest! Do you want to get on the stage where there is lots of glamour and money? Do your ego and mass opinion nag you to create when otherwise you would be happy just dancing? Are you full of ideas for social reform and the drama and bored with abstract dancing?

Just liking to dance is such a simple reason for doing it that it is often ignored. For myself, I did like to. Not being bothered about content my first group dance might have been named anything, but was actually "Greek Mourning Dance"[1] because it was in natural movement—only the Greeks were [thought to be] very natural when I was very young and [supposedly] moved in a circular form like a ritual. The joy I had in devising the interlocking patterns and the making of something magical from many girls moving ceremoniously has lasted me for years. This first phase of dancing for the love of it went on for a long time. It was a wonderful experience just to learn the folk and art dances of most of the peoples of the world from Ruth St. Denis and Ted Shawn, and from original sources. Also I had a chance to experiment with my creative powers, and to present these efforts to thousands of people on tour with them—these were golden days for a young American dancer. The path is not so easy now, either economically or artistically. Gone are the days when tours were eight months long, dances were primarily good theater, employment was for the year round, and generous directors who offered an audience and a stage, night after night, to company members who could contribute originality.

In this period, I composed dances that were extremely popular and widely imitated because of their striking character. In fact, none of the dances I have done since have had the theatrical brilliance of my *Hoop Dance, Scarf Dance* and *Soaring*. I last heard of *Soaring* being

[1] The actual title was "Greek Sacrificial Dance."

done on skates in an ice review, and hoop dances used to abound even in Japan.

I think it is significant that these dances all had props as their feature. Was this not an unconscious urge toward an extension of movement and something more then a stagy trick to engage the eye? In this period, however, there was no movement or talk of composing, no rules or principles for it whatever and the theater eye of the director was the sole judge of the results. The process was very simple: you had an idea for a new number, you worked it out and showed it, after which you were told whether it let down in the middle, was too long, needed a surprise ending or a better climax. I have no quarrel with this way or with the judgment of experience, nor with just "doing a number" from the basis of talent combined with trial and error. In fact, I have hardly deviated from this approach to the present day. But I have an unusually good perception of form in all its aspects, which is not the good fortune of many. Most young dancers need help from the knowledge of principles, which only analysis can give them. I amused my hearers very much one time by confessing, after an hour's demonstration of composition theory, that I do not use this method at all, and that my dances just come to me.

6
New Dance

As far back as I can remember, group activity has always fascinated me. My early impressions of games are not connected with the participants so much as with the audience—the surge and mass-uplifting and the concerted cry. I remember also the wheel and sweep of birds in flight, the endless counterpoint of people walking on the streets, and once a battalion of ventilators across the roofs turned rhythmically with the wind, as from one enemy to another.

From whatever source came this liking for the interplay of units moving together, I know that it gave added point to my conviction that it is only the group composed of individuals which can say anything significant or stirring about contemporary life. Comment on our times through group dancing has always been my sole aim, even though the work I do today may seem quite different from what I did when I gave my first recital in New York apart from the Denishawn Company.

The aim had to wait until I was able to build a new technique. I feel that the old technique was foreign in every way to the world we live in and must be discarded. Therefore, the early dances had to be confined to experiments with form and movement. For me this consisted of rediscovering and reapplying the natural laws of movement to group composition. The ballet group has been based on the [aristocratic] social scene of which it was a part. The leading dancer was either king or queen, the next important dancers served as all the ranks of nobility, and the *corps de ballet* was just as unimportant as "the rest of the people" were at that time.

Modern dancers began their work within the social setting of democracy. There were leaders to be sure, but the group, which corresponded with the *corps de ballet*, grew in increasing importance until now group action is far more important than solo action. Even my earliest dances stressed the group and used the individual entirely in relationship to that group. This was really a difference between a democracy and an empire and obviously required a complete reorientation. New forms had to be discovered which could express concerted action and replace the [hierarchical] system of the ballet.

It is only within the past two seasons that I have been able to take that form and use it in its largest sense. Dances on the recital stage were considered long if they occupied ten or twelve minutes; the usual dance was about five minutes long. But the new trilogy I have composed, which includes *Theatre Piece*, *With My Red Fires* and *New Dance*, requires an evening and a half for presentation, unless I had occasion to do it as Eugene O'Neill's *Mourning Becomes Electra*, beginning in the early evening. In these three dances I have been able to take the forms I had been experimenting with and mold them together in the same way as a symphony. Since I was primarily interested in commenting on social experience, the purely abstract form would not do. I combined it with drama. These are no longer recital dances; they are theater dances.

I had an accumulation of things to be said which could no longer be confined within the limits of a short dance. There was the whole competitive modern world in upheaval; it must be expressed and commented upon and it was too large a theme for fragments and episodes. Whether it was my personal life within this world or my sense of technical sureness that impelled me into these three dances is difficult to say. I believe it was both. In almost the entire dance world I had seen nothing but negation. Anyone could tell you what was wrong but no one seemed to say what was right. It was with this mental conflict that I approached *New Dance* first, determined to open up to the best of my ability the world as it could be and should be: a modern brotherhood of man. I would not offer nostrums and I could not offer a detailed answer. It was not time for that, but it was time to affirm the fact that there is a brotherhood of man and that the individual has his place within that group.

When I had stated this in *New Dance*, I could return to the theme of life as it is: in business, in sport, in the theater and in personal relationships. This I did in *Theatre Piece*. When I had finished these two, the first in symphonic form, the second in dramatic form, there was still one element missing to round out the picture. These two had treated of social relationships and there still remained the theme of love, of the relationship of man to woman. This too is a universal theme, even though the modern cynic is inclined to scoff at it. This I treated in *With My Red Fires*.

It is easier to describe this more-encompassing form in a specific case than in theory. Let me describe *New Dance* briefly. It was, of course, the dramatic idea that dictated the form throughout the dance. It was generally to be a dance of affirmation, progressing from disorganization to organization. The group was to be at first an audience. To suggest this, I used an arrangement of blocks in the corners of the stage, upon which they stood as though at an arena, unconvinced but interested. Within this arena, Charles Weidman and I opened the dance. When we had stated our themes it was necessary for me to draw the women into my orbit and for Mr. Weidman to draw the men into his. This was a partial integration but could not be completed until the two groups had been fused. When this had been done, there was a combined group dance of celebration. This was a group integration but I was not satisfied to leave it at that point. The group, though fused, was still composed of individuals, and the last section of the dance was devoted to an expression of their personal themes in relationship to the group. Naturally, since all members were participating, there was no longer any necessity for an arena; there was no audience. For this last section, then, and the only place in the dance where the action was momentarily broken, the blocks were moved into a pyramid in the center of the stage to focus the action and stress this unity.

In the *Prelude*, since I wished to convey a sense of incompletion, I chose the Broken Form, by which I mean an unfolding continual change, with contrast but very little repetition. (This is the same form that Mr. Weidman and I used in *Rudepoema*, where a movement was done several times and then discarded, giving way to a new one.) By this means I was able to present the main themes of the whole composition, which were later elaborated in *First Theme*, *Second Theme*; and *Third Theme*; fused in *Processional* and *Celebration*; and re-expressed by members of the group in *Variations and Conclusion.*

The movements used in the *Prelude* were by no means spontaneous. I had a very clear reason for them. Since the main direction was to move from the simple to the complex, from an individual to a group integration, I consciously eliminated any free use of the hands, arms, head and torso. I concentrated on feet and leg themes, which were the first to be used in the primitive dance and folk dance. The conscious use of the other members of the body was a sophisticated development at a much later time. Therefore, until the group integration had been achieved, the feet and leg themes seemed more correct and expressive.

These were developed in the following three sections called *First Theme, Second Theme* and *Third Theme* through the two essential movements of the body: the change of weight and the breath-rhythm. Each of these three had to have a loose form, broken, unbalanced, not symmetrical, and must have an inconclusive ending, since each was a fragment of a whole. In the sequence of dramatic idea, no conclusion was reached until *Processional* and *Celebration.* Each part merged into the other, therefore, in form as well as idea.

For these the Broken Form would no longer do. Those themes that had been stated were to be conveyed to a group, and a group never accepts immediately en masse. It must be swayed and inveigled and molded; it both refuses and accepts. For the *First Theme,* then, I used the Cumulative Form [in] which only gradually by accretion the whole group comes to perform the theme.

Processional uses the Cumulative Form once more and in movement brings the themes to a head; in dramatic idea brings the whole group to an integrated whole. I chose a slow tempo for this because it gives a sense of greater control and, theatrically, is obviously in sharp contrast to the preceding sections. It was here, too, that I used symmetry for the first time as the best way to express cohesion and completion.

The groups have now fused and break into a *Celebration,* which is built in fugue form, joyous in character. The fugue was eminently suitable to express a harmonious chorus wherein no member was more important than another. It is a short theme and goes directly into a square dance, which is again consciously symmetrical. I could have used several symmetrical forms here, but chose the square dance because at a moment of climax, forward movement is the most powerful. Other forms do not have that direct impact.

Having thus unified the men's group and the women's group, one more section was necessary. Too many people are content to achieve a mass-movement and then stop; to me it is too cold a regimentation. I wished to insist that there is also an individual life within that group life. The dancers here work in a line in a whirling-star pattern around the central pyramid. I could have allowed the two lines to remain in one place to form a path for the new dancers who now come in and perform briefly their own personal themes. However, by having this line whirl and by having the new dancers enter from different directions, monotony was avoided and a greater space and excitement was achieved. In this *Variations and Conclusion,* I used the Repetitional Form where the group performs the same movement over and over. The brief solos were in Broken Form against the *basso sostenuto* of the group.

Fusion of various forms within a single work can, I believe, broaden the field of modern dance and give it a new life and a new potency. Solo dances flow out of the group and back into it again without break, and the most important part is always the group. Except for an occasional brilliant individual, I believe that the day of the solo dancer is over. It is only through this large use of groups of men and women that modern dance can completely do what it has always said it would do.

New Dance and the other two works that I have not described are no longer a series of episodes strung along in a row. They are a cohesive form in the way that a symphony is and need neither music nor story as crutches to support them. Both *Theatre Piece* and *With My Red Fires* treat more specific details in dramatic form, even to the degree of having roles, but they are always stated in movement, not in acting as we know it in the theater today.

I like to think of this as a new form of theater, using all the materials that belong to the theater. Three acts of words spoken from various divans and chairs seem too often sterile. "Actions speak louder than words" may be a trite phrase in its present usage, but nevertheless it has the approval of modern psychology, indeed of all modern thought. The purpose of the modern dancer is to shape and form that movement into vital drama.

7

The Relationship of Music and Dance

My point of view

I come to the dance and music, both of which are my dearest loves, from the theater. I have a theatrical point of view about both of them and this is a very special point of view. I admit that it is a biased point of view too, because music and dance have certain special characteristics which they must have in order to fit into the theater. So I like the music that supports the aims of the theater. The theater's aims are, very briefly and very generally, to arouse emotion. We go to the theater, we see the play, we hear the opera, we see the dancing to be aroused, to feel. So as a consequence of this, I am prejudiced in favor of music that arouses emotion. Thus you will be able to put me in my category, whatever you think it ought to be, and judge my preferences for music. I like music that evokes feeling.

The theater arouses, or should arouse and seeks to arouse, feeling. And dance shares in this, and the kind of music that is appropriate to the theater has to be this kind of music too. Flaubert put it in these words, very succinctly. He was thinking of audiences, what audiences want in the theater. He says, "Make me laugh, make me cry, amaze me, delight me, exalt me, make me love, make me hate, make me think." And please note that "make me think" is last. This is not the important part of the list. Because an art that only makes one think is doing badly what science can do extremely well. So that I don't agree with someone like Stravinsky, for example, who says, "The tonal masses are to be regarded objectively by the ear." This is not the kind of music that we in the theater can feel is appropriate.

Rhythm

I like music that relates to thinking, feeling and doing of people. I think of this as of two kinds: music that is both rhythmic and melodic, or rhythmic and vocal. These seem to be the first two forms of the art expression of people. Even before there were human beings, in the animal world there was dancing and there was singing and there still are. Birds have courting dances, and beating and fluttering of the wings go along with this; and bird song is one of the delights of the natural world. The insect world has group dances, one of which I based a ballet on, *The Life of the Bee.* This has been described by Maeterlinck in his book as being very well organized, highly geometric and with many figures in it, and is a prime example of rhythmic movement in the insect world.

Who hasn't enjoyed the unfolding of a flower in the slow-motion camera, with its accents that are not smooth, which do not flow openly, smoothly, as would seem to the naked eye? The camera reveals that this has a rhythm, that this has accents and pauses.

And also, who hasn't been delighted by the symphonic complexity of a summer afternoon out of doors where the trees and the grasses and the clouds and the flowers and the water are all under the command of the wind, almost like a conductor with a baton? The shadings and the timings and the accents are all in different speeds, all in different dynamics and with different time lengths: a fascinating and highly complex organization of rhythm in nature. Indeed, the scientists tell us that inanimate Nature itself is a vast rhythmic structure of vibration from the atom to the galaxy of stars. Some of these vibrations are too long, too extended. We cannot possibly understand the rhythm of the glacier. The time spaces are so extended and so cosmic we cannot possibly grasp it. We can only grasp all of these rhythmic ideas if they are within the span of our own human perceptions.

It seems to me that rhythm and vocal sound are born right in us. They come to us from untold ages past. And I think, also, that they were the very first arts and they were extant long eons before recent inventions like painting and architecture, language and sculpture. Music (the vocal kind especially) and movement have been linked from the very beginning. They were handmaidens; one accompanied the other. The song was the expression of the emotion, perhaps, of the dance; or the dance expressed one kind of emotion and music accompanied it. For twenty or thirty thousand years this wedding of the two arts has certainly existed.

But then there was a change. Roughly by the Middle Ages the two arts seemed to be pulling apart, and they have been pulling apart more and more. They are concerned with their own techniques, with their own theory, with their own procedures. They tend, first of all, not only to drift apart, but also to forget their origins, to forget their heritage. The musicians ignore the physical basis of rhythm and dancers are much too insensitive to music. They not only forget their common origins but their interdependence. Each is concerned with craft, technique, theory. My branch of the art, theater, is not even a good partner to music, nor the music to dance as good a partner as it could be, because of this tendency to divergence, to concentrate on the isolated problems of each art itself.

I'd like to explain what I mean by lost origins. Take rhythm as an example. Rhythm, it seems to me, can be defined as measured energy, grouped into patterns. How do we perceive this measuring and this energy and these patterns? Through the body. All physiologists and psychologists agree that this is so. Rhythmic perception is gained from sensation through the tensions of the muscles and activity of the body and this, by the way, is a special sense of the body. It has been named: it is called *the kinesthetic sense.* It is a sense added to the five with which everybody is familiar and it is the sense which measures energy, which tells you where you are in space, which judges the amounts of tension, of accent, of time-space, of all things which have a bearing on rhythm.

This kind of rhythmic sense does not come from mathematics. The mathematics comes from it. So that rhythm is not ¾ time and ¼ time on paper. That's a code for the eye to remember these rhythmic sensations. Nor does rhythm come from words, such as *accelerando, ritardando, andante, allegro.* These are also code words to remember the rates of energy that the body has already perceived. I believe that out of the rhythmical structure of movement has grown the rhythmical structure of music.

I would like to make two very simple examples of this. Supposing we had been developed not from the monkey family as we were and finally had grown up to stand on two legs and to free the hands for other uses. Suppose we had developed from the fish family. Suppose we were by now super-fish instead of super-monkeys. We would have an entirely different sense of rhythmic structure. The fish has no idea of beat. There is nothing in his physical makeup, in his organization to make him aware of beat. The fish rhythm would be undulating. We would have faster and slower and we would have been aware of time-space, but the accent, the beat idea would have been quite foreign. I don't think a fish, even a super-fish, would ever be aware of or get any feeling of continuity from the tick of a clock. They are not conscious of anything of this sort in beat. The beat comes from the fact that we are bipeds. Men have walked from time immemorial. There was a binary accent of rhythm in 2/8 time and the feeling of the beat I think comes from the walk, the run, marching, dancing on two feet. The sense of beat comes not only from that, but also from the heartbeat and from other stresses and accents which we use to grasp things, to pull, to strike, to make sharp or smooth accented movements, measured in energy.

Now there is one other example. How do you think we have gained our conception of slow and fast? What is slower? Slower than what? What is fast? Faster than what? We use these terms in all sorts of situations in human activity, of course in music too. It doesn't seem to me that this is from marks on the metronome. It seems to me that this is from the walk. Everybody has a point of reference in the body itself, so that the walk is what we think of as the common denominator when we say faster. We are unconsciously thinking faster than the normal walk or slower than the normal walk. And anything which pushes us beyond that into a faster tempo than the walk or the heartbeat is faster than anything which retards us, which feels slower. Now, let me show you, as an example, without thinking of this in musical terms at all. Just think of this in the sense of reference to a slower or faster beat. This would be one: [handclapping] clap – clap – clap – clap – clap. This would be a little slow, I think. The beat of the walk is probably about like this, everybody's common denominator of the walk: [handclapping] clap – clap – clap – clap – clap – clap – clap – clap – clap. This feels about in the middle of beating tempos. The next is fast, because it is faster than the normal walk: [handclapping] clap – clap – clap – clap – clap – clap – clap – clap – clap – clap – clap. Now this one: clap – clap – clap – clap. This gets so slow it isn't a rhythm at all. We begin to lose the continuity between accents and it begins to be without a beat. There is accent and then a pause. It loses its connection or its grouping with the other beats; so slow, so far away from the normal rhythm of a human being that it doesn't seem to be a rhythm at all.

Now if it is true, and I believe it is, that rhythm is perceived in the body, then dancing is the best training for encouraging and improving this sense of rhythm, because it is the one activity that not only includes the physical but also the mental and the emotional equipment of the human being. There is total physical awareness but also these added elements that do not occur in the practice of sports or in any other physical activity that I know of. Havelock Ellis, the eminent British philosopher, has said in *Dance of Life*, "If we are indifferent to the art of dancing we have failed to understand, not merely the supreme manifestation of physical life, but also the supreme symbol of spiritual life."

I do not say that a musician would be without rhythm if he did not dance. This is obviously not true, because a great many musicians have a very fine sense of rhythm, both in the best sense and in the overall sense of the flow of rhythmic phrases. I think that this is because there are a great many individuals who have an instinctive remembrance of these origins of rhythmic movement in the body.

But I do say that a musician who does not cultivate the body is overlooking the source and the regulator by which rhythm is perceived. In other words, it could be improved, it could be developed where there is none, it could be very much better.

The conductor is the most physical of all musicians. I am always interested in the kind of dance the conductor is going to do on the podium. The moment he gets in front of his orchestra he begins to use body rhythms immediately to make his meaning clear to the orchestra. He moves, he gets up on the half-toe, he sways the body, makes motion—all expressive movement in the body. This is the only person among musicians who is completely free and completely able to use the body. He isn't tied to an instrument.

I think that dancers are very lacking in some aspects of rhythmic and musical training too. They do have rhythm and phrase sense, but they often do not have good enough ears to relate the movement accurately enough to what they hear.

The phrase

One more part of music I want to speak of which has its origin in the body, and that is the phrase. The phase is born of what originally was said, or sung, or spoken on a breath. It seems to me that our sense of the phrase, just as our sense of the beat comes from the walk, comes from the long-ago origin when people spontaneously sang or spoke on a breath. We instinctively like this kind of phrase. The phrase that is in a normal breath-length or even slightly elongated, as the singers use it, is satisfying. It is a comfortable phrase. The phrase that is longer than that is apt to make us feel slightly tired. We're trying to catch up; we don't feel we can take a breath because the performer isn't taking a breath. I think we find this in literature, too. I myself am absolutely exhausted at the end of reading one of Faulkner's page-long sentences.

The too-short phrase also is not satisfying. It doesn't seem to be complete. We're not borne along with it. We have some breath left which hasn't been used, so the very short phrase seems to be too sudden, too accented, too broken off. We could learn very much about the phrase. The dancers could too, especially. I'm making a very radical suggestion now: I think that dancers should be taught to sing, and I don't mean *solfeggio* and I don't mean just the ordinary song. I mean in the sense of using the voice freely and almost improvisationally, the way it was when our primitive ancestors were making the first song. This would give us a whole new sense of phrase. And I think this wouldn't do the musicians any harm either, not to be merely confined to the conventional song but to learn to flow, to rise in feeling through the voice and to realize the length of the breath. And in this connection I'd like to pose a question: why do you think the conductor in rehearsal sings the phrase to his orchestra? It is because it isn't on the page and also because very often it isn't in the musician either. But he has the feeling, he is the dancer-conductor.

8

Doris Humphrey Speaks to Students

The problem of projection

By projection I suppose we mean how do you convey the meaning or the mood of what you are doing to the best possible advantage to the people who are in front of you? How do you accomplish this? Projection has a lot of different facets, particularly for modern dance. I don't think it is such a problem for ballet, because the ballet has a long tradition of movement by which the body has been trained to show its best line or its most provocative movement in the proper direction so the whole impact of it is immediately apparent. But modern dance has a different premise, that of improvisation and choreography of an original kind; so the problem of projection really has to be reexamined as a part of the technique of performing.

First of all we have to remember the picture-frame stage. Communication comes from only one direction. Whatever you are saying in movement has to be stated so that there is the greatest possible projection in this one direction. This seems very obvious, but it's something that young dancers are very likely to forget. Perhaps the most important thing one could say about projection is that there certainly will be none unless there is conviction back of what you are doing. Unless you believe in yourself, no one else will, I assure you. The tentative dancer, the one who is afraid or is very uncertain, either of his movement technically or because of the theme, cannot project. The body is extremely revealing. It tells us more than speech, more than almost any kind of communication what is really felt, what is going on in the inside; so that without the conviction, there is automatically very little projection.

That is number one. But there are technical aspects to this. You can believe in yourself thoroughly and have all the assurance in the world, but if you do your dance in the wrong place, for instance side to side against the back wall, it is not going to convey very much power. The stage is an area that is divided into different sections with dynamic differences according to where you are. If you are going to do something that you want to make very personal, then it should be brought forward, very close to the edge of the stage where we get the impact of the personal equation. It would be quite wrong—you would have great difficulty in making this carry to an audience if you were to put it way back in the corner or way back against the side. There are many technical know-how points to remember about where to put your dance.

Then there also is the question of the line, and where the face is and what it says. I am one of those who believe that the face is the most expressive part of the body. Other parts are communicative and expressive too, but the face is the part of the body we are most used to reading. When you meet people you talk to the faces, you glean the meaning of the conversation by the responsiveness of the face. One does not watch the hands or the body very much, one watches the face. So it seems to me that unless the movement is backed up with a face, the most eloquent and familiar part of the body is lost. The face will tells us what the feeling is, whether it is one of grief, exultation, or happiness more quickly than any other part of the body. I am afraid many young dancers do not realize this. They work impersonally in class and then they are suddenly called upon to do some kind of a dramatic movement in a particular dance; the movement may be very expressive, but the face is still the impassive one of the classroom.

Projection must take into account the architecture of the theater and the relationship of the audience to the performer. We are, at the moment, in a conventional kind of theater, an orchestra floor that has a little rise, a balcony above. If you are going to project down to the first few rows, those in the balcony are going to see nothing but the top of your head. The face has to be raised to an unnatural degree, and the whole line of the body too, much higher than in the conversational level. One of the most amusing and also, I think, instructive illustrations of this is in some of the old movies. I am thinking of one of Sarah Bernhardt in *Camille*. She stands in a doorway at the back of the stage about to make an entrance into the room. She leans on the door with her head lifted high, communicating her sense of imminent tragedy not to the actors in the room with her, nor to the orchestra, but to the balcony, thereby taking in the full sweep of the theater. This was part of the grand manner of the day and much of this seems dated, but the high projection is still valid.

One more thing about projection, namely about the line. Because of the one-sided stage we have, this picture frame, box-like stage, not just any body lines you can think of will do; to be effective they should be only those which will carry to the front. For example, if you stand in profile with the arms extended to the side, you have lost most of the design. The line of the arms is invisible, and the whole movement becomes a wasted effort. I don't mean that you should always dance facing front and stare at the balcony. By no means. This would be quite wrong. Sometimes a dramatic situation demands a communication between people. This may often mean that you don't look up and out at all. But almost any movement can be altered slightly so as to project it with the greatest possible impact in the line, even in scenes like this.

Subject matter

There are hundreds of things to dance about beginning with your own experiences. There are also hundreds of things that you shouldn't dance about. There are both do's and don'ts: the don'ts would include too intellectual concepts that do not lend themselves to movement, scientific subjects. I got a letter from a dancer the other day about the peaceful uses of the atom bomb. How can you dance about the atom bomb? The subject would have to be put into some specific situation. It would have to be concerned with some reaction of people to the bomb and this would put the emphasis on feeling, and if the idea of "bomb" could be retained at all it would be minor. You can't dance about scientific subjects. There are also plots from literary sources that are too vast for the dance. It is all very well for the movies to attempt Tolstoy's *War and Peace*, but I wouldn't like to see a group of dancers try this. There are limitations.

In general, it is a good idea to dance about something you understand. Don't feel that in order to be different or to be original you must fasten on something very remote from what you know about. If we are going to promote American dance, then we had better try to work indigenously, that is, foster what we have and try to understand that better, rather than go far away for thematic material.

Denishawn, and on how it started in the dance world

I was brought up in Chicago, and then when I was eighteen my family moved to a suburb. That was Oak Park (where I was born and where I returned right after high school). I began teaching; it was necessary to earn a living, I had had some ballet training by then, some ballroom dancing and whatever passed for aesthetic dancing, and clogging and gymnastic dancing. It is probably a little hard to realize that not too long ago there was no such thing as modern dance. I studied ballet with an ex-Viennese ballet mistress who was in Chicago. Her name was Josephine Hatlanck [sic] and she taught with a stick and high button shoes. So I had what there was, and by eighteen I was fairly accomplished and began teaching children and ballroom classes.

This was doubtless the most unhappy time in my life. I thought I was going to be buried alive in Oak Park, Illinois, because there did not seem to be any way to be released from the drudgery of teaching in a small town and, of course, like all young dancers I wanted very much to dance.

The opportunity came with Denishawn, and the reason it came is another point I want to emphasize. I had a wonderful teacher [Mary Wood Hinman], and a wonderful teacher is some thing that you should cherish when you find one. This teacher not only had vision, but was interested in the whole field of dance. She used to go abroad and bring back whatever seemed to be of value. She also had an individual interest in her students and I was one of those she advised and encouraged. It was she who brought the Denishawn School to my attention. [The school] was on the West Coast at that time, so I went out to Los Angeles and never came back to Oak Park. It was one of those very fortunate things; it was the right time and the right place for me.

I had by this time a very flourishing school of my own in Oak Park, but fate made it very easy for me to get away. At Denishawn was another teacher who was looking for a school, a place to settle. She wasn't from Oak Park, but she was interested in getting something to do that was secure, and she didn't mind small towns—in fact she liked them. So I handed her my school; she went back to Oak Park and I went on with Denishawn. They were fascinating years, and this was the first time that I had ever been able to step my foot on a professional stage which had been the goal and the objective for such a long time.

Then, of course, there were the magnetic and stimulating personalities of the two leaders, Ruth St. Denis and Ted Shawn. I think everybody who has ever been with Ruth St. Denis has come away with a little of her vitality and her spark. She was a magnificent person. I think that we didn't learn too much from her about dancing, because none of us who were with her has really gone on as she did. She was at her greatest in Oriental dancing and also in religious dance. But what we did gain from her was vision. Here was a woman who saw the dance whole, complete. She was not interested in a little segment, but in all of it, and was a major influence in inspiring the future leaders of American modern dance.

It was like a university of the dance at Denishawn: we did absolutely everything. Any kind of dance that they could lay their hands on we had some part of, which included American Indian, Spanish dances with roses and a black wig, and Hopi dances with squash blossoms and the legs all done up in white wrappings. We did American folk dancing, Japanese, Siamese, Burmese, the world's dances. After a while it began to seem a little scattered. I felt as if I were dancing as everyone but myself. I knew something about how the Japanese moved, how the Chinese or Spanish moved, but I didn't know how I moved or what the American heritage should be. As dancers they [St. Denis and Shawn] had a different point of view; they felt that all dance was universal, the common property of all dancers. But it came to me and, I think, to a good many others who were with them, that it was imperative to find out what we were as Americans and as contemporary dancers. This led to a break, of course, and to a completely new start.

The life of the dancer at that time was so different from the way it is now. I had the incredible luck of going to the Denishawn School, immediately going into their company and touring year after year after year, and then teaching in between; so that there was not question of [earning] a living; everything was ready and provided.

This succession of performances of the Denishawn Company went on for something like ten years, but there was one break. After I had danced with them for several seasons there was a shift in their policy and what they were doing came to an end and they didn't have a new plan ready. So, all of a sudden I was faced with nothing—no Denishawn, no company, no school anymore. It was in Little Rock, Arkansas, that I gave the last performance with the company. Then what? Well, I had $100 saved in my pocket and I went back to Oak Park where I still had some pupils who were pretty good. I got together four girls and some dances and costumes and I rented some scenery and got an agent. I bought five tickets for them and myself to open in Detroit in vaudeville on $100.

This was way back—then you could do it. And of course vaudeville was a familiar outlet for me because I had played with the Denishawn Company in vaudeville for years on the Keith circuit, the Orpheum circuit, the Pantages circuit, two-a-day, three-a-day, four-a-day, even five-a-day. This was by no means unusual. Vaudeville was a wonderful experience. Too bad you don't stand a chance to try it! You learn, first of all, discipline. Now, for a concert to begin five or ten minutes late is standard procedure, and if you are not quite ready between dances, they'll hold the curtain for you. There was nothing like this in vaudeville. You learned to be exact, you had to be there. The curtain went up, and if you were not there they played the music anyway, and nobody cared except the manager who came tearing back from the front and said, "Where is so and so?" There was no such thing as holding the curtain.

[St. Denis and Shawn] were very generous; they gave me and other people solo work. They composed dances for me, and they also allowed me to compose dances of my own and present them on their programs.

Some practical advice for the young dancer

Everybody wants to dance, just as I did. I know you do. I know that all young dancers in all the studios want to dance. How are you going to do this now? First of all, I think it is very unlikely that you can do anything alone. There are a few I know who have made a name for themselves and are able to function alone; that is, they have a studio and settle themselves in it, work all alone. This is the most difficult way to do it and the least likely to make a success unless you are a genius, and genius is scarce. This is apt to strike the young dancer as being very desirable, because the ego is very strong, [as is] the sense of independence. You think, "I'll do something by myself; I've got ideas." The surge of youth and vitality leads you to make this error sometimes, but I don't believe it will work very well.

I think that the only way we can hope to find some success for young dancers in the concert field is in collaboration of some kind. Either you should collaborate with each other in small groups or affiliate yourself with an institution or a company that has some opportunities to offer. It hurts me to see some young dancers, who are so eager to perform, accept some of the sporadic things that are offered. Maybe an individual dancer decides to give a concert once a year and gets a group of people together who probably have not worked with her before, who do not understand her approach. They all work like dogs and then give the concert, and that's the end of it. This is not what I mean by collaboration. I mean a collaboration with a plan of continuity.

There are opportunities for small ensembles, small groups, two or three or at the most four, in this country where individual initiative would count for something. It won't count for much if you go off and bury yourself in a studio. It's a big country, and there are lots of colleges and institutions of various kinds where there are dates to be had. You must plan realistically. The way not to do it, it seems to me, is to aim with a hammer. You are going to strike New York City with what you have. You are going to do a whole program with your choreography. And you're going to put it on for one performance. The result will be, first of all, that you will lose money because everybody always goes in for too much rehearsing, too much costuming, too much music, too many dancers. Also, you are likely to win the disapproval of audience and critics; there are very few young dancers who can sustain a whole program with just their pieces and their ideas. Young dancers don't have enough resources to hold the attention.

Now there is, of course, a difference between the audience in New York and that in the rest of the country. This is a very sophisticated audience. They see absolutely everything. What would not be acceptable here is acceptable there very often.

One of the saddest things, I think, is to be a drifter in this field. If you go from studio to studio looking for something you have never quite found, and you never stay in any place long enough to make a mark, then you have no one really to help you, no one to advise you or to be concerned about what becomes of you. You are always a new student and you don't stay long enough to form any attachments. I am a great believer in alliances, in planning, in cooperation. My advice is: don't try to do it alone; don't try to do whole programs by yourself. Get other people to collaborate. They will supply new ideas and more audiences.

This is all about dancing on the concert stage. There are other ways of functioning as a dancer. There is the teaching field. There is show business, there are ballet companies and there is television. These all have varying degrees of value. One of the most important and rewarding of these is teaching, and there are many opportunities all over the country. But I have had very little success in persuading young dancers to leave New York and go to Nebraska, for example. They say, "Oh, me go to Nebraska? I want to stay here, something might happen in New York!" There are good positions out there and it is not nearly such a desert as you might think. The rest of this country has a lot of intelligent people in it and one of the great advantages is that you are going to be one who knows the most wherever you go. There, all the opportunities, whatever they were, would gravitate toward you in the studio, the theater, or in the university. You can't all dance here, it's impossible. Somebody has to go away.

Isolation and egocentricity

When I was young my personal experience tended to isolate me and the people I was with a good bit from other dancers because, as I said, we went on very long tours—one-night stands all over the country. When you are traveling like this, you don't see anybody else, you rarely hear about any other dance that is going on. Therefore, under such circumstances, it was very difficult to even keep track of what others were doing, let alone be concerned with it. However, there really isn't much reason to be isolated now, even when you travel a great deal.

Now all are very well conversant with what goes on in the field, and there should be a greater sympathy and a greater interest and action than there is. We must not tend to discount any kind of modern dance in which we are not personally concerned—"Mine is the only kind!" This viewpoint is very narrow and destructive. We had better have more concern for the whole field, or we won't have any field.

Do not listen to isolationist kinds of talk or reject or ignore other dancers or movements; resist such influence for the good of the whole. Do not forget: you are the ones who are going to be responsible for carrying the work on.

Part 2

NOTES ON DANCES

1

Sonata Tragica

1926

The ensemble flowering of dance, instrument of as much depth, color and architectural capacity as the symphony, although as yet possibilities have only been scratched. Solo instrument always greatest importance. I believe that music and dance are exactly analogous in that the solo and ensemble bear the same relationship to each other. Technique: succession based on natural flow found in nature applied to whole body.

Music: Edward MacDowell

2

Color Harmony

1928

Following my theory that any abstract idea can be danced, I chose *harmony* . . .[1]*

First a cool blue waltz—then a yellow rhythm, warmer and capricious—thirdly a red rhythm rich and sturdy, always attracted in turn to blue and yellow. Each time red goes by they each blow toward them like flowers—and each time the attraction grows stronger, until one red, brave and more lustful than the rest, captures a trembling and vibrant yellow. Immediately they begin to spin, and a burst of orange, a silk scarf, flames up from between them. All the rest are hardly a minute later, and all the reds and yellows are in an ecstatic whirl of orange to the horror and disdain of the cool blues. Some are vibrating so rapidly that their very ardor flings them apart, and both yellows and reds sweep down upon the blues who attempt to escape and run hither and thither distractedly. But they are caught one after the other—and immediately are encircled by flames of green or purple. The couples spin so closely together they are as one—madly, with long swoops and dips—often interfering with each other. There is no form—only vibration. Through the wild colors shoots a silver arrow—it separates the couples—it draws them one by one into form. All the flaming colors are laid down in rhythmic patterns in a pyramidal form, up high steps to a climax, where a silver streak molds itself into a stream of light that goes up into infinity.[2]

Each of the three primary colors moves according to its own being; the red is both sensual and scintillating; the green moves soothingly; the purple is rich, threaded by an aspiring violet. As each color follows its own course, it is inevitably flung against another, and as each collision occurs a new color suddenly emerges—the confusion becomes greater and rapidly draws toward chaos and death. Through the maelstrom appears a silver light, symbolic of a controlling intelligence, which draws all the flaming colors into the rhythmic harmony of its own essence.[3]

Music: Clifford Vaughan

* Superscript numbers throughout this section refer to the sources of the notes (see page 136).

3

Etude Patetico

1928

This duet is in a dramatic key, romantic in a sense that the dance expresses personally-felt emotions but abstract in the sense that the drama is suggested in movement, not pantomime.

Music: Alexander Scriabin

4

The Banshee
1928

In Gaelic folklore, every Irish family has a "banshee," who is a bearer of departed souls. To hear the wail of the creature around the housetop is to know that someone is to die and the louder the wail, the nearer is death.[1]

I had a small green screen, fixed like a chimney, around which I oozed and wailed.[2]

I'm . . . covered in a moldy green, head and all, and try to move like a lost soul.[3]

Music: Henry Cowell

5

Water Study
1928

This lovely dance is done without musical accompaniment and depends entirely on the rhythmic flow of the bodies of the dancers for its power and continuity. The composition begins with gentle wave undulations, rises to a strong climax and subsides again to calm. This dance was one of the first to be done without music and has helped to prove that the dance is an independent art.

Probably the thing that distinguishes musical rhythm from other rhythm is the measured time beat, so this has been eliminated from the *Water Study* and the rhythm flows in natural phrases instead of cerebral measures. There is no count to hold the dancers together in the very slow opening rhythm, only the feel of the wave length that curves the backs of the group.

Performed in silence

6

Air on a Ground Bass

1929

The old air is done in a modern way with only a suggestion of the antique. The dancers are more concerned with the nobility and graciousness of the style than with period manner. Written in 1645, the music is arranged in a quaint way, the "air" making patterns around the soberly reiterated "bass."

Music: Henry Purcell

7

Life of the Bee

1929

For the bees, the individual is nothing. The queen's existence is conditional only and she is, for one indifferent moment, a winged organ of the race—her whole life is an entire sacrifice to the manifold, everlasting being whereof she forms a part.

Her one thought is the accomplishment with untiring sacrifice of the mysterious duty of the race.

The pitiless duty of the hive, in which the individual is entirely merged in the republic and the republic in its turn invariably sacrificed to the abstract and immortal city of the future.

In the Holy of Holies of the palace lies the adolescent princess who awaits her hour wrapped in a kind of shroud, motionless and pale, and fed in the darkness.

Long and mysterious war-cries the adolescent princess sends forth during the combats and massacres that precede the nuptial flight. The workers are dancing, beating their wings that appear thus to generate the necessary heat and accomplish some other object besides . . . for this dance contains extraordinary movements so methodically conceived that they must infallibly answer some obscure purpose.

Original music: Pauline Lawrence
Later music by Paul Hindemith

8

Descent into a Dangerous Place

(originally entitled "Gargoyle")

1929

This fantastic creature has the utmost difficulty in finding its way home. Through crevices and broken rocks it slips and slides—a most perilous descent even for a supernatural being. The music is written in dissonant harmony by the contemporary composer, Adolph Weiss, and forms a fitting accompaniment for the creature's angularities.

Music: Adolph Weiss

9

Alcina Suite

(co-choreographed with Charles Weidman)

1929

This suite of dances from the opera *Alcina* are modern interpretations of antique form—gently satirical, they preserve the balance and symmetry of the classic, while making use of contemporary style.

Music: George Frederick Handel

10

Speed

1929

. . . the illusion everyone has experienced that rapidly moving objects are almost static. So the theme is: the more speed, the less effort.

Music: Unknown

11

Drama of Motion
(originally titled **"Motion Concerto"**)
1930

This experiment has no program, no music, almost no costumes. In positive terms, it has three contrasting qualities expressed both in movement and design. The first, *Processional*, is slow and sustained, moving with a warm strength in its curving flow. The intricate patterns weave about the stage for the purpose of pleasing the eye with an ever-changing series of lines and spaces.

The second part, *Transition*, is a brief dance which modulates from the slow movement of the first part to the sprightly jiggling of the second. There are surprising accents and odd quirks and jerks, with the solo keeping a remnant of the first movement through it all.

The third movement, *Conclusion*, opens with a thundering rush of power through the bodies of the entire group. This powerful accent is reiterated in different ways until a contrasting, delicate quality emerges. Rudely, the first theme returns and sweeps up the group, bursting beyond the limits of the stage in its crude gusto. The last spurt of power spends itself in a fall circling the stage.

Performed in silence

12

Parade

1930

The reaction of a crowd to a parade.

Music: Nikolai Tcherepnin

13

The Shakers

1931

The subject is fascinating to read about—but is chiefly important as a starting point for the composition. The subject is never the point. . . .

The real name of this sect is the "United Society of Believers," but its members were called *Shakers* by outsiders who saw the meetings of this strange group. The Society flourished on the east coast of America during the 1800s and 1900s but died out. They believed that sin was a substance that could be shaken off the hands like a liquid. This shaking process took a rhythmic form, and men and women were strictly segregated on either side of a chaste line in the meetinghouse. The whole took on the form and aspect of a religious and exotic dance.

The ritual as performed by the Humphrey-Weidman Company begins with a rapt swaying of the believers and emerges into a rhythmic dance punctuated by revelations of the Holy Spirit in scriptural language. Led by the eldress they are at last purified and cleansed of sin in bursts of hysterical flying and jumping.

Music: Traditional, adapted by Pauline Lawrence, based on Shaker hymns

14

Two Ecstatic Themes: Circular Descent and Pointed Ascent

1931

The first part is in circular and spiral movements, soft and sinking to convey a feeling of acquiescence.

The second part, in contrast to the first, moves in pointed design to a strident climax suggestive of aggressive achievement.

The whole is a counterpoint of circular and angular movement representing the two inseparable elements of life as well as of design.

Music: Nikolai Medtner and Gian Malipiero

15

Dionysiaques

1932

The bull-god was the great deity of Cretan civilization, and periodically, a great celebration took place in his honor, on which occasion a priestess was offered to him as a sacrifice. This was done in a curious and spectacular way which forms the theme of the ballet.[1]

My ballet *Dionysiaques*, although stemming from ancient days, is a modern psychological drama about ourselves. Being an American I am party to our morbid liking of spectacular danger, that is the Dionysian passion for unbalance, and this characteristic expressed in original movement makes the dance veracious.[2]

Music: Florent Schmitt

16

Suite in F

1933

Prelude—a formal series of greetings by the dancers to each other and the audience, followed immediately by the

Sarabande—in which the men, at first dominant, yield the stage to the women, who dance a short bacchanalian passage giving way to the

Gigue—a celebration of the ever-recurring new life led by the men dancers in the form of an ancient tree worship and Maypole dance.

Music: Albert Roussel

17

The Libation Bearers

1934

Brief Synopsis

1) Funeral dance of Electra and the chorus over the murder of her father.
2) Entrance of Orestes and his lament over the murder of his father.
3) Greeting dance of Electra and the chorus and the beginning of the plot for vengeance.
4) The plot to kill Clytemnestra who has been convicted of the murder of her husband.
5) The consecration before the altar to the task of avenging their father's murder.
6) Dance of Electra and the chorus to incite Orestes; Orestes goes within to accomplish his task.
7) Return of Orestes with the bloody crown and veil of Clytemnestra. Dance and song by the chorus: Hymn of Justice. Orestes is already overcome by remorse, but Electra dances with the chorus a triumphal march.

Music: Darius Milhaud

18

Duo-Drama

1935

Duo-Drama represents in abstract form the struggle for supremacy between man and woman. The opening section, "Unison and Divergence," pictures the two moving harmoniously together, absorbed in the joy of rhythmic effort. Gradually the greater vitality of the man, beyond the reach of the woman, results in the first break of their unity. The continuing phrases find the woman developing her own individual expression and attempting to fit into the man's original pattern, which he has resumed. Failing in this, there is a complete break between the two and the man is left alone to dream of a woman nearer his heart's desire. She appears as the incarnation of this dream in the next movement, "Phantasm," romantic and fragile, then disappears, leaving him alone as before. In the last movement, "Integration," the woman reappears, sure of her own identity. The struggle for supremacy is repeated followed by an eventual understanding and harmony.

Music: Roy Harris

19

New Dance

1935

In its design it is a development from a broken, groping beginning to a conscious, balanced, rectangular conclusion. It is the growth of a conception, vague at first, in form, but with vitality and enthusiasm in its loins. This form gradually emerges more clearly, more and more definitely, until the movements have a fixed and controlled pattern. This work also has overtones of drama. It is the life of the blessed among the world's people. The blessed are the dancers, the world's people are everybody else. The blessed set about making a pattern for living in which each one has a place both alone and with others; a place to be himself without any curtailment of his powers and with full use of those powers.

Music: Wallingford Riegger

20

Theatre Piece

1936

This dance depicts the world as it is today: a place of grim competition. I have called it *Theatre Piece* to stress the fact that, even though this savage competition is dominant at the present time, it is far from being the whole of life. It distorts and kills too much of life that is good and erects symbols and numbers and figures in place of human values. Throughout the dance, I play the part of one who rebels against this way of life and prophesies a better way of living.

Prologue: The roles are assigned to the various dancers so that, as in a theatre within a theatre, they may enact this partial, abortive life. In the next five sections, different phases of modern life are shown.

Behind Walls: The first scene the actors show has to do with business, where brokers, stenographers and businessmen are seen in wild competition. One figure above the rest controls them like a dictator and directs their transactions and money-changing as though they were inhuman puppets. Here, and in the remainder of the dance, I dance the part of a rebel.

In the Open (Hunting Dance): Here we see the methods of business carried over into daily life. The stenographers and shopgirls put on their hats and go out from their place of business at the end of the day. When they find a man, they exhibit themselves and have a great struggle to see which shall get him.

Interlude: In a brief lull when the forces of competition are quiescent, I, in revolt against the world as it is, dance a theme of harmony and peace. The movements are prophetic of *New Dance* in which the ideal world is depicted.

In the Stadium: Everyone is champion here, whether defeated or not. The dance shows football and golf; the same repeated movements; the same crowds doing the same things and all reacting at the same time, as they sit eagerly awaiting a "thrill."

**In the Theatre:* Again there is competition of one actor against another. They make fools of themselves in order to curry the favor of the crowd that seems slightly bored at their antics. At the least ripple of applause, they all bob up and down like loose-jointed puppets.

The Race: Having presented this competition, this grim race for livelihood, in four daily activities, I attempt to bring this idea to a climax in this section. All of these various aspects are fused into the single fact that underlies them all: a race made breakneck and pointless.

Epilogue (The Return): My rebellion is carried to a climax. The group is suddenly brought out of its theatre-acting with a realization of something new and better. The dance ends on a hushed note of expectancy.

Music: Wallingford Riegger

* Choreography for *In the Theatre* by Charles Weidman

21

With My Red Fires
1936

For the divine appearance is brotherhood, but I am love
Elevate into the region of brotherhood
With my red fires.

—William Blake

When thought is closed in caves,
then love shall show its roots in deepest hell.

—William Blake

The soul drinks murder and revenge
and applauds its own holiness.

—Doris Humphrey

First a hymn to Aphrodite, or Priapus or Venus, anyway to the excitement, the greatness, the rapture, the pain of, frustration that is love. A voice will speak of that from a temple and the ever-willing victims will respond with flutterings, stabbings, listenings, impatience, fire in the blood. Next the process will begin. Put the force to work, seek out the mate, rush from one to the other, buffet the rest out of the way. Yes, there are two lovers at last, the end is all but achieved, the heat and thirst quenched. But what and who is that beckoning in the window? It's a woman—old—she's beckoning to the girl lover—she's the mother—she says it's late and not time for young girls to be lugging around with unknown young men and goodness knows who he might be or what sort of a family he comes from. Come in this moment, your virtue is at stake, the world will say you're a bad girl. You won't? You will do as I say. Sew the seam, mop the floor, walk like me, talk like me, come away from the window—How can I mop the floor and sew the seam with my lover outside? I have danced in the Hymn to Priapus and I belong to my love—The old one is quiet now in the house, steal away through the window to the waiting lover. In the shadows find him, wrap him round. The old one has missed you, she's screaming now from the top of the house, the alarm is spreading, people are running, shouting, they are on the morbid scent, they gleam with virtuous hate. She's run off with a nobody? Which way? To the town, to the inn? No, here by the wall. Tear them apart, the dirty things. What shall we do, old one, marry them with a gun and giggles or run them out? See that they're well battered, punish, pinch, tear, beat, and I shall shut the door. So—let's take them over the rocks, up-down through the rocks, leave them at the Priapic stone.*

Music: Wallingford Riegger

* This is a preliminary outline of the dance. The final version, with its references to militarism, lynching, self-destructiveness and the eventual triumph of the lovers differs from this. *Ed.*

22

Race of Life

Adapted from a cartoon by James Thurber

1938

The particular characters in this family fantasy are types of ordinary Americans who, through the extraordinary imagination of Mr. Thurber, are exaggerated to his taste. They go through a set of adventures symbolized by Indians, ghosts and other strange creatures, which are certainly no stranger than the mad world we really live in. Underneath the farce-comedy spirit, however, is a lesson about the race of life toward empty riches that is as sober as the moral in an Aesop fable.[1]

Notes on the ballet *Race of Life*

The scenario is based on a set of cartoons by James Thurber. It shows the adventures of a family, mother, father and child, in the process of striving for success. At the opening the child carries a flag which says EXCELSIOR, and which eventually the family manages to plant on a mountain top. In the meantime various delays and encounters occur. The father has an illicit meeting with a Beautiful Stranger. The whole family is beset by Indians and later by Night Creatures. There is also a satirical Spring Dance that precedes the final race to the summit.

The style of the ballet closely follows Thurber in mood and appearance.[2]

Music: Vivian Fine

23

Passacaglia in C minor

1938

This famous *passacaglia,* originally a court dance, has been treated as an abstraction with dramatic overtones. The minor melody, according to the traditional *passacaglia* form, insistently repeated from beginning to end, seems to say "how can a man be saved and be content in a world of infinite despair?" In the magnificent fugue which concludes the dance, the answer seems to mean "be saved by love and courage."

The *passacaglia,* originally written for organ, is composed in two parts on an eight-bar theme stated at the opening. The second part is a four-voice fugue.

I compose in two ways, in dramatic form and abstract form, depending on the subject matter I wish to convey. The famous *Passacaglia in C minor,* by Bach, is one of a series of abstract dances inspired, in this case, by the need for love, tolerance and nobility in a world given more and more to the denial of these things.

Bach's music, to me, is the cry the artist hears today: "How can a man be saved and be content in a world of infinite pathos?"

Music: Johann Sebastian Bach

24

Square Dances

1939

A gay suite of familiar dances in the spirit of a party. There is a square dance that keeps coming in like a refrain, and duets for each couple include a country dance, a tango, a schottische and a waltz. Neither the steps nor the figures have more than a nodding acquaintance with the originals—they are, in fact, inventions like variations on an old folk song. What has been retained intact from the traditional is the spirit of dancing together for fun.

Music: Lionel Nowak

25

Variations

1940

These short pieces are known as abstractions, but this is misleading, as anything done by a human being must mean something. Sometimes the dancers "talk" to each other, sometimes to you, but most of all they are telling something about themselves, for nothing so reveals human nature as gesture, and dancing is gesture set to music.

Music: Lionel Nowak

26

Song of the West

1940

The first dance (*The Green Land*) expresses the quiet joy and rolling sensuality of green fields in the sun. The second (*The Desert Gods*) has for its theme the desert in which the sun shines with a magical intensity. Bounding the scene are mountains, rocks, great slopes and the enormous bowl of the sky. The figures moving in it are symbolic of the burning light and are also sometimes people of the desert moving in a ritual hymn to the sun.

Music: The Green Land, Lionel Nowak;
The Desert Gods, Roy Harris

27

The Land of Ing ("ings")

(A Children's Entertainment)

1941

I.

Let's imagine a land of Ing
and a king of the Ings called Lee.
His true full name was Leap-ing Light
But "Lee" for short was he.
He had three dancers in his court
To teach the others how
To do the simplest steps in time
And how to speak and bow.
Here are the Ings, they're enter-ing
They're walk-ing on the beat
They'll meet and bow, and show you how
They dance in the Land of Ing.

II.

The youngest Ing could run like fire
And never lose the beat
Runn-ing had springs in both her knees
No one so light and fleet.
Fall-ing knew how to relax
From standing to the ground
She showed the others how to drop
Without a scratch or sound.

Turn-ing thought it fun to spin
Round and round and round
Did she get dizzy? Not a bit
There is a trick she found.
(What is it?)

III.

The King enjoys a just renown
For jump-ing like a cat
He's up – he's down, he'll lose his crown
Leap-ing as high as that.
We're go-ing, go-ing, go-ing
And it's very nice to know
We've all had one more chance
(…) runn-ing, leap-ing, turn-ing, bow-ing
(…) in the dance.

Music: Lionel Nowak

28

Four Chorale Preludes

In Thee is Joy,
Man's Fall from Grace,
Love and Mercy Shall Restore Thee,
Awake the Voice is Calling
1942

Specifically as to Bach, I intended the *Chorale Preludes* to be a naïve and stylized miniature, greatly simplified and understated, of the respective rewards of unity and disunity in human behavior.

Music: Johann Sebastian Bach

29

Partita in G Major

Preambule, Allemande, Courante, Sarabande,
Tempo di Menuetto, Passepied, Gigue

1942

Bach, whose humble admirer I am, thought it was fun to do a set of these partitas on odd Sunday afternoons, and two centuries later people, and even dancers, are entitled to have fun, too.

Music: Johann Sebastian Bach

30

El Salon Mexico

1943

The set: A raised square platform about center, a curved runway leading from it and a bench downstage right, two small blocks up stage right, two small blocks up stage right, tall screens set at varying angles surround the whole. As different playing areas are used, the scene suggests a room for a rendezvous, a garden, a winding street, a ballroom, an amusement park.

The form: The choreographic plan, loosely devised on the theme in the music, concerns the adventures of the central figure, a Mexican peon. He is seen first alone, moving in a dream-like sequence in the center of the platform where he meets the first figure of the fantasy, a peasant girl, slender and exquisite. As this passage fades, a group of noisy and blatant girls entrance him. He dances with them all as though in a ballroom, he the only partner, the only lover. Sounds of a festival procession interrupt. Two girls with decorative play-sticks appear weaving their way toward him. He joins them in their dances, and arriving at the fiesta engages them in crude horseplay. The romantic opening passage then recurs with the peasant girl. Suddenly all the women appear, previous scenes seem to be jumbled together. He senses the end of his dream. In a forte conclusion, he retreats to his original position, while the women vanish by twos and threes. He is left clinging vainly to his first love, who also disappears as the last notes sound.

Music: Aaron Copland

31

Inquest

1944

Based on a London newspaper account of an actual coroner's inquest in mid-nineteenth century England, the story concerns a poor cobbler and his family, who tried to stave off bitter poverty and keep their miserable home together. They are thwarted by the terrible social conditions of the time and their humble life is sucked out from under them by overpowering circumstance. Deprived of their basic human needs, the son goes blind and the father dies. The verdict of the inquiry into the cobbler's death pronounces the cause to be simple starvation.

It was John Ruskin, in his book of essays *Sesame and Lilies*, who first delved into this particular case, examined it on moral and social grounds and expressed his personal vehemence at a society that could allow such inhumanity.

The work, however, is couched in the values of the theater. It speaks not only of social injustice but also of individual anguish. It is not only angry; it is also compassionate.

The first section is a bare but poetic pantomime drama of the story of Mary and Michael Collins and their son. This action is keyed in a quiet tone and takes place in the Collins' garret home. Around this home is suggested the grim movement of people in a slum street.

As the family enacts its personal drama, the narrator reads the background material on their lives unearthed by the coroner's inquiry. Then the verdict is given and the second section begins.

This is a group dance that enlarges the spare movements of the pantomime into an emotionally cumulative drama involving a large ensemble. In this way the grief and tragedy of the small family group are heightened into a rebellion of larger dimensions and more universal meaning.

Music: Norman Lloyd

32

The Story of Mankind

Adapted from a cartoon by Carl Rose

1946

Our hero is a sensible creature who knows that a life with substance needs a nice bit of property somewhere, something a man can see and stand on, and a biggish house solidly built to make him feel important and safe in a world of fools. He needs a substantial woman to put in it, too. Once having decided on this as an additional requirement, he finds it rather amusing to add the fashionable quirks and curlicues she thinks up, even contributing ideas of her own to keep him dazzled.

Our couple begins roughly about 50,000 B.C. in the most distressing cave without style or plumbing, but soon our man recognizes housing as a proper concern of solid people and embarks on a rapid career of building through the ages, ever more impressive, permanent and pretentious. This should take us about fifteen minutes to dispose of, after which we come to the denouement. One fatal day, our hero and heroine, sitting in their dizzy penthouse poring over plans for the house of the future, find the walls of stone and steel shivering with a message. The papers say, and the radios say, we are going to have a War, an Atom War. There is nothing for it but to rummage in the closet for that old cave they used to have. So we take leave of our friends, safe, snug and bewildered in their ancient but serviceable abode.

Music: Lionel Nowak

33

Lament for Ignacio Sanchez Mejias
1946

This is a dramatic version of the poem *Lament for Ignacio Sanchez Mejias* by Federico Garcia Lorca. Lorca was, before his death during the Spanish revolution, Spain's leading poet and dramatist, and his *Lament* is considered his finest work. The poem concerns the life and death of an Andalusian bullfighter of great prowess and beauty, and was chosen by José Limón because of its power and intensity.

Edwin Honeg says of the Spanish poetry:

> *(It is) alive with characters whose feet are aching to dance, whose voices at every turn are breaking into inspired Song.*

The poem is in four parts, each of which depicts a different attitude toward the death of the bullfighter Ignacio, ranging from the impassioned utterances of the beholder to the formal elegy of tribute. Since these two expressions of the theme are marked, the dramatization provides two women to speak the poetry: one, a fateful and impersonal figure who records Ignacio's destiny; the other an anguished observer of the well-loved hero. The formal introduction that precedes the actual poem serves to introduce the three characters, "Ignacio," "Guardian of Destiny" and "Witness and Mourner," in their dramatic relationships. Because of the special significance with which all Spanish poets, and especially Lorca, view blood, and the spilling of it, the three are bound round by a red thread which symbolically entangles the Man, his Fate and his Mourner.

The entire poem has been cut extensively in the interests of pace, clarity and dramatic impact; the actual wording is a compilation from many translations. The entire conception has been pointed toward a more inclusive meaning than is strictly indicated in the poem—the keynote is in the lines of the last part:

For you are dead forever
Like all the dead of the whole earth,
Like all the dead who are forgotten.

The drama of the bullfighter is intended to signify the struggle of all men of courage who contend in the ring of life and who meet a tragic end, to which they are bound by destiny, and to which they must go alone.[1]

My attitude to the use of words with dance is that they must form a collaboration, each staying within its own orbit. I see words as a means of conveying facts, and the dance as the means of expressing emotion. Of course the word can be eloquent in describing feeling too, but in a fusion of the two arts, I believe the feeling should be the function of the dance and the words should convey whatever we need to know about place, time, state of being, or any fact which the dance, by its nature, cannot express.

All the poet's vivid words of a descriptive nature are left to stand alone, once the emotional reactions to these things form the choreographic structure. It is not intended to be a dance *per se*, but a theater piece, a synthesis of the dramatic arts.[2]

Music: Norman Lloyd

34

Day on Earth

Man's Work and First Love, The Family, Loss and the Refuge of Work

1947

Notes by Letitia Ide[1] (edited)

The female group seen as the curtain rises is composed of a square-shouldered woman (the earth mother), a child (the child to come) and a charming young woman (the man's first love) whose journey in life is about to begin. This group, Doris told us, should have the quality of a Henry Moore statue of a family. I felt, in my position as the mature woman, that serenity can be shown with legs quite widely spaced, and the arms close to the body, parallel, and resting on the legs with one hand turned up and the other down. The eyes are looking out, dreaming about the child that will come in her future.

On the other side of the stage is a young man making plowing and seeding motions, advancing toward the young woman. Meeting, they dance a duet, and then she runs off. From that point on, as the mature woman rises and leans toward the man, spreading her arms and her scarf, her attention is almost continuously on him. One feels the joy of the beginning of a great love, plus the euphoria of a most perfect summer day. Two sharp high accents with the right arm have an ecstatic quality as the man and the woman move forward with arms overhead, alive with in-out breath pulses. Her arms lift to the man with a sudden intake of breath. The woman's left leg extensions and arms in a wide, full pattern are as if encircling the earth. A rich, warm rounded style is called for throughout.

At the end of the duet, the man and woman join together with hands meeting in what I think of as a kind of pledge. They turn upstage in the silence, approaching and uncovering their waking child.

In the section that follows, play with the child is sometimes interspersed with work movement of the adults. At one point, the mother goes away suddenly on a trip or an errand. The child is momentarily lost and lonely, but turns to the father and establishes a new relationship before her mother happily returns. The family has a joyous time together, until at the end when the mother has a moment or two of foreboding about the time when the child will leave home (she drops out of the little up-and-down jumps sooner than the others). After the final game, the child moves upstage and back under the parents' arms as they try to catch her. She moves in a final circle as the mother tries to take her back, thus turning a game into a sad reality. The child rises from a final crouching position with her arms moving, one at a time, in a slow circling movement parallel to the floor, denoting the passage of time. She moves offstage, her eyes on her parents, her left arm lifted in farewell. Her parents move slowly but steadily downstage opposite and sink to the floor.

The lament, following, is a combination of direct movements of anguish with sharp arm thrusts slanted in the direction of the child's departure, with slow, sorrowful stretching and lifting movements and breath releases, like cries, coming from the solar plexus. There are brief remembrances, quickly over, of their earlier life. The man is supportive of the woman through most of the lament, but at the end, in conflict, she breaks away and falls.

She rises, turns front, and opens her arms with an outstretched scarf, all in one continuous phrase. The whole sequence should be smoothly moving with only two small accents of the arms with the breath. The woman folds the scarf down over her chest with a final fold high in the air, and she lowers to the ground as life seems to drain out to the earth with a dreamlike, other-worldly, floating quality.

Music: Aaron Copland

[1]Letitia Ide, a distinguished member of the José Limón Dance Company, originally danced the role of the Mother.

35

Corybantic

1948

1. (Agon) Beyond the edge of the Known lies the terror of the Unknown: the Enemy. In the contest with him, all reason is engulfed by passion.
2. (Pathos) Ritual of survival and communion
3. (Satyric) Discovery of the Unknown and celebration

Note: Korybant, in Greek mythology, is celebrant of a rite given to wild and destructive dances.[1]

1. *Assai lento, allegro molto* Maelstrom of panic
2. *Lento, ma non troppo* Resurrection
3. *Allegro non troppo* Carnival of unreason

A vision of our time: the dilemma of the man of good will beset by fear and panic.[2]

Music: Bela Bartók

36

Invention

1949

The title, borrowed from music, indicates the statement of development of non-programmatic themes in movement terms. In four parts, consisting of a solo, two duets and a trio, each in a different mood.

Music: Norman Lloyd

37

Night Spell
(originally titled "**Quartet No. 1**")
1951

Things of the night riding the wind beset the Sleeper. Before terror can entirely take him, he gropes toward waking, trying to re-order the menace of nightmare into remembered love and comfort.

Music: Priaulx Rainier

38

Ruins and Visions

1953

Ruins and Visions, inspired by a poem of Stephen Spender, is a dance-drama of contemporary times. The theme is the attainment of tolerance and understanding through mutual suffering in a catastrophe. The time is just before the Second World War.*

In the opening scenes three classes of people are introduced, all hostile to each other. First, a mother and son, aristocratic and arrogant; second, three actors isolated in their make-believe world; and third, three street urchins, crude and insolent to those not of their kind. Each of these three themes has a development within its own orbit only to be violently disrupted by the impact of war. In the words of the poet

The storm rises
The walls fall, tearing down
The fragile life of the interior.

In the crisis of loss and suffering it is the artist, symbolized by the actor, who is most able to understand and comfort the unhappy people of the play and bring them to a common vision of survival. With him as catalyst and leader they take the first tentative steps toward a united destiny.

Music: Benjamin Britten

* Although Humphrey has set the dance to take place before World War II, the costuming and set for the dance place it before World War I.

39

Felipe el Loco

1954

Felipe, a Spanish gypsy, was brought from his homeland to a cold, gray northern country to coach a group of dancers. They proved to be incomprehensible to one another in every way. The resulting clash seemed to unbalance the mind of Felipe, who was known thereafter as "Felipe the Mad." (This dance, based on a true story, was suggested by Dr. Alfred Matilla.)*

Music: Jorge Gomez, Carlos Montoya, Andres Segovia

* The story as described by Cyril W. Beaumont in *The Complete Book of Ballets* is: "During a visit to Seville, Diaghilev visited a gypsy dance festival; one of the dancers, a youth known as Felix, impressed him greatly, although when not dancing he was of sullen disposition and even a little unbalanced. Diaghilev realized the boy's value as a source of material for his new ballet [*Le Tricorne*, or *The Three-Cornered Hat*] and engaged him to teach his steps to [Leonid] Massine. The youth assented eagerly, believing that he was to be the star of the production in preparation. When, later, he was disillusioned, the shock was such that he grew strange in his manner and ultimately became mentally deranged."

40

Airs and Graces

1955

Seventeenth and eighteenth century music abounds in graces, mordents and embellishments of various kinds, for which there is a large and picturesque vocabulary. That is used here, not as technical descriptions of music, but for the mood and meaning of the words.

Music: Pietro Antonio Locatelli

41

Dawn in New York
1956

Based on poems by Federico Garcia Lorca

Cast: Black doves, Young man, Sign of spring, Workers

The New York dawn has
four columns of mud
and a hurricane of black doves . . .
"The dawn comes and no one receives it in his mouth . . .
"they know they are going to the mud of figures and laws,
to artless games, to fruitless sweat."

—From *The Dawn*

What signs of Spring
do you hold in your hand?
A rose of blood
And a white lily.

—From *Ballad of the Little Square*

Music: Hunter Johnson

42

Theatre Piece No. 2
A Concerto for Light, Movement, Sound and Voice
1956

PART 1 In the Beginning

PART 2 Ritual

PART 3 Satires from the theater

a. Actors, first dialogue, second dialogue

b. Dancer

c. Singer

PART 4 *Poem of Praise*

PART 1 In the Beginning

PART 2 Ritual

Parts 1 and 2 suggest the origins of theater and the lighting of the fires of drama at the altar of ritual.

PART 3 Satires on the distortions of theater

PART 4 *Poem of Praise*, uses of the four theatrical elements

(Part 3) Satires from the Theater: Actors first dialogue[1]

HE: Do you remember the morning—when we walked out from La Citta di Roma—and over that long hill . . . and on the hill the thought—went out, into the horizon—like the horizon coming back into the thought.

You looked at me, and I looked at you—and there we stood—looking—far into the horizon as it looked into us.

And then? And then, what?

SHE: You said to me—"Come, dear, we'll go together toward the horizon"—and where did we go? Toward the horizon? Not at all—backward—outward—inward—everywhere excepting toward the horizon.

And it became so that I couldn't stand it any more . . . I had to go my own way . . . so did the horizon . . . We both went our own way. You went your way . . . and where are we now . . . Tell me!

HE: Here—there—and nowhere. . . .

SHE: You think you can hurt me? You think you can do me in? But no matter how much you try—I am going to take you and I will break you in little pieces with my little fingers—Yes, I can do that—because—I have the moral superiority—the psychological firmness . . . and the will . . . to do you in!

(Part 3) Satires from the Theater: Actors second dialogue

HE: Darling (echo: darling, darling, darling)

SHE: Sweetheart (echo: sweetheart, sweetheart, sweetheart)

HE: I love you (echo: I love you, I love you, I love you, I love you) Darling, sweetheart, love (echo: darling, sweetheart, love)

Darling, I know that you are here—and that you would like to recapture but ah, I don't know—do you really think so? Do you really think so?

SHE: No, no—not now—not now.

HE: But if we can't go back to La Citta di Roma then where can we go? Where can we go?

SHE: Let's stay here, let's stay right here.

HE: But it's all so dull and boring—insufferable—I can't take it anymore—I must leave—I must leave . . . this place.

SHE: If that's the way you feel go your way—I'll go mine.

HE: I don't like it and I won't take it. I said I won't take it!

Now you can go your way—but don't stop my hand—It's all tosh and pifflewit and you get out of it all just what you are—No more, no less. . . .

I said what you are . . . no more, no less. . . .

Go back the way you came—go in where you came out. . . .

Now I've had enough and I mean enough—you've made the worst in me come forward and the best drop out. You can go back to your horizon—get behind or into it—and if you like it take it with you as long as I never see the damn thing again. Goodbye.

Poem of Praise[2]

O light, the spirit that leaps
from the eye of the sun to every
living eye
O Light, dwell in us.
Light, kernel of all fruits and
Seed of every flower
Light, wine of the bone of beast
And man,
navel of the earth,
and jeweled span of all the
planets
Orange of the East,
Purple of the West,
Tranquil light, garment of the air
Fierce light, costume of the flame
Green skin of sea and grass
Gold hair of the harvest land.
Praise the Sun!
Praise the Moon!
Praise the Earth!
Praise the names of all things
And praise the voice that calls
All things into being.

—May Swensen

Music: Otto Luening

Sources

Note: In the following list, the source "Doris Humphrey Collection" is housed at the Library for Performing Arts, Jerome Robbins Dance Division, New York Public Library, Lincoln Center, New York.

Part 1

1: My Approach to Modern Dance, in Frederick Rand Rogers, *Dance: A Basic Educational Technique.* New York: The Macmillan Company, 1941.
2: Doris Humphrey Collection.
3: *Spur* magazine, date unknown.
4: Unpublished interview, date unknown. Collection of Charles Humphrey Woodford.
5: Doris Humphrey Collection.
6: ibid.
7: ibid.
8: Speech to students of the Dance Department, Juilliard School of Music, November 7, 1956.

Part 2

Sonata Tragica: Doris Humphrey Collection.
Color Harmony: ibid.
Etude Patetico: ibid.
The Banshee: 1, Doris Humphrey Collection. 2, in Selma Jeanne Cohen, editor. *Doris Humphrey: An Artist First.* Pennington, NJ: Princeton Book Company, 1995. 3, ibid.
Water Study: Doris Humphrey Collection.
Air on a Ground Bass: ibid.
Life of the Bee: ibid.
Descent into a Dangerous Place: ibid.
Alcina Suite: Collection of Charles Humphrey Woodford.
Speed: Doris Humphrey Collection.
Drama of Motion: ibid.
Parade: program note, Lewisohn Stadium Concert.
The Shakers: Doris Humphrey Collection.

Two Ecstatic Themes: program note.
Dionysiaques: 1, Doris Humphrey Collection. 2, *Trend* magazine, 1932.
Suite in F: program note, Lewisohn Stadium concert, 1933.
The Libation Bearers: Doris Humphrey Collection.
Duo-Drama: ibid.
New Dance: Collection of Charles Humphrey Woodford.
With My Red Fires: Doris Humphrey Collection.
Race of Life: 1, program note, Tufts College, 1940. 2, Letter to Dean Frederick Prausnitz, The Juilliard School, November 2, 1955.
Passacaglia in C minor: Doris Humphrey Collection.
Square Dances: program note, Tufts College, 1940.
Variations: program note, 1940.
Song of the West: program note, 1940.
The Land of Ing: Doris Humphrey Collection.
Four Chorale Preludes: letter to John Martin, *The New York Times* dance critic, 1943.
Partita in G major: letter to John Martin, January 23, 1943.
El Salon Mexico: Collection of Charles Humphrey Woodford.
Inquest: ibid.
The Story of Mankind: Doris Humphrey Collection.
Lament for Ignacio Sanchez Mejias: *Dance and Dancers*, March 1959. In Selma Jeanne Cohen, *Doris Humphrey: An Artist First.* Pennington, NJ: Princeton Book Company, 1995.
Day on Earth: José Limón Foundation archives, with permission of Timothy Ratner and Stephanie La Farge.
Corybantic: 1, program note, American Dance Festival, 1948. 2, program note, American Dance Festival, 1949.
Invention: program note.
Night Spell: program note.
Ruins and Visions: Doris Humphrey Collection.
Felipe el Loco: program note.
Airs and Graces: program note.
Theatre Piece No. 2: 1, program note, The Juilliard School, April 1956. 2, program note, American Dance Festival, 1956.

A Short Biography of Doris Humphrey

Doris Humphrey (October 17, 1895–December 28, 1958) was born in Oak Park, Illinois, into a family with deep roots in New England as educators and Congregational ministers. Her grandfather, descended from Elder William Brewster (of the Mayflower), was Reverend Simon James Humphrey, District Secretary for the Interior of the American Board of Foreign Missions of the Congregational Church. Her maternal grandfather, Reverend Moses Hemenway Wells, served as an instructor, principal and as a superintendent of schools in various New England private and public schools. Both men were graduates of Andover Theological Seminary, which had the purpose of training missionaries. Her mother, Julia Ellen Wells, was a graduate of the New England Conservatory and an accomplished pianist.

Doris's childhood home was The Palace Hotel on Chicago's north side, which her parents managed and which catered to a theatrical clientele. Her education was at the progressive Francis W. Parker School from which she graduated in 1913 as one of the first students to complete all thirteen grades.

The school's philosophy embraced the principles of instilling creativity, attention, mental and physical expression, independent thinking and social responsibility. Part of the curriculum was dance instruction taught by Mary Wood Hinman, who recognized Doris's talent and who would become her early mentor. Her dance training up to the point of graduation included ballet, folk, ballroom and aesthetic dancing.

By the time she was eighteen, Doris was an established teacher of children and ballroom in Oak Park and other Chicago suburbs and was beginning to choreograph dances for children with the encouragement of Mary Wood Hinman. But her aim was to be a performer, not a teacher. So, at Hinman's suggestion she enrolled in a Denishawn School summer course in 1918. There, Ruth St. Denis told her the words she longed to hear: "You shouldn't be teaching, you should be dancing."

She quickly became Denishawn's star performer as well as its prime teacher performing in vaudeville and on a two-year tour of the Far East between 1925 and 1927. Although encouraged by Miss Ruth to choreograph her own works, including *Soaring*, *Valse Caprice*, *Hoop Dance* and *Sonata Tragica*, she left Denishawn in 1928, together with her partner, Charles

Weidman, to search for ways to express a contemporary American spirit in dance. It was during this formative period of modern dance in the late 1920s and early 1930s that she developed her theories of movement and composition, began to write about them and to tour the country with the Humphrey-Weidman Company doing what she called "missionary work" in the family tradition, but for the cause of modern dance.

Between 1928 and 1944 she performed and choreographed for the Humphrey-Weidman Company such works as *Water Study, The Shakers, Air for the G String, New Dance, With My Red Fires,* and *Passacaglia in C minor,* all of which can be said to relate to the theme of harmony expressed in her Declaration (Chapter 1 in this book). When physical disability ended her career as a dancer, she turned entirely to composition, serving as choreographer and artistic director for the José Limón Dance Company. Three prominent works of this period are *Ritmo Jondo, Day on Earth* and *Night Spell.* She was also on the faculties of the Juilliard School, the Bennington College Summer School of the Dance, and the American Dance Festival and was head of the Dance Department at the 92nd Street YMHA in New York City.

During her final illness, she recorded her principles of choreography in *The Art of Making Dances,* widely used by generations of dancers as a reference and textbook.

From early pieces that mirror the movement of winds and waves to mature compositions that reflect the complexities of human relationships, Doris Humphrey's choreography continues to be performed throughout the world.

Bibliography

Anderson, Jack. *The American Dance Festival.* Durham, NC: Duke University Press, 1987.

Cohen, Selma Jeanne. *Doris Humphrey, An Artist First.* An autobiography of Doris Humphrey, edited and completed by Selma Jeanne Cohen. Pennington, NJ: Princeton Book Company, Publishers, 1995.

Humphrey, Doris. *The Art of Making Dances.* Hightstown, NJ: Princeton Book Company, Publishers, 1987.

King, Eleanor. *Transformations: A Memoir, The Humphrey-Weidman Era.* Brooklyn, NY: Dance Horizons, 1978.

Kriegsman, Sali Ann. *Modern Dance in America: The Bennington Years.* Boston: G.K. Hall & Co., 1981.

Siegel, Marcia B. *Days on Earth: The Dance of Doris Humphrey.* New Haven and London: Yale University Press, 1987.

Stodelle, Ernestine. *The Dance Technique of Doris Humphrey and Its Creative Potential.* Princeton, NJ: Princeton Book Company, Publishers, 1978.

Videography*

Dance Works of Doris Humphrey, Part 1: *With My Red Fires* and *New Dance*
Performed by the American Dance Festival Company
DVD and VHS 60 min., color

Dance Works of Doris Humphrey, Part 2: *Ritmo Jondo* and *Day on Earth*
Performed by the José Limón Dance Company
DVD and VHS 60 minutes, color

The Doris Humphrey Technique: Its Creative Potential
Written, directed and hosted by Ernestine Stodelle. Contains performances of *Air for the G String* (with Humphrey), *Quasi-Valse, Two Ecstatic Themes* and *Etude Patetico.*
VHS 45 minutes, color/b&w

Charles Weidman On His Own
VHS 60 minutes, color/b&w

The following Doris Humphrey Legacy DVDs and videocassettes include coaching, analysis and performance:

The Doris Humphrey Legacy: *Air for the G String*
VHS 90 minutes, color

The Doris Humphrey Legacy: *The Call and Breath of Fire*
Performed by Nina Watt with the José Limón Dance Company
VHS 63 minutes, color

The Doris Humphrey Legacy: *The Shakers*
DVD 91 minutes, color

The Doris Humphrey Legacy: *Two Ecstatic Themes*
Performed by Sarita Smith-Childs of Momenta Performing Arts Company
VHS 90 minutes, color

The Doris Humphrey Legacy: *Water Study*
VHS 91 minutes, color

* All DVDs and videocassettes listed here are available from Princeton Book Company, Publishers (www.dancehorizons.com) and Amazon (www.amazon.com).

Organizations dedicated to preserving and performing the works of Doris Humphrey

Doris Humphrey Society
605 Lake Street
Oak Park, IL 60302
www.dorishumphrey.org

Doris Humphrey Foundation for Dance at Goucher College
1021 Dulaney Valley Road
Baltimore, MD 21204
www.goucher.edu/dhfd

Doris Humphrey Institute
mgn@dorishumphreyinstitute.org

Doris Humphrey Foundation UK
www.dorishumphreyfoundationuk.co.uk